NORTH AMERICAN DINOSAURS

ANKYLOSAURUS

ANASTASIA SUEN

Rourke Educational Media
A Division of Carson Dellosa Education
rourkeeducationalmedia.com

ROURKE'S
SCHOOL to HOME
CONNECTIONS
BEFORE AND DURING READING ACTIVITIES

Before Reading: *Building Background Knowledge and Vocabulary*

Building background knowledge can help children process new information and build upon what they already know. Before reading a book, it is important to tap into what children already know about the topic. This will help them develop their vocabulary and increase their reading comprehension.

Questions and Activities to Build Background Knowledge:

1. Look at the front cover of the book and read the title. What do you think this book will be about?
2. What do you already know about this topic?
3. Take a book walk and skim the pages. Look at the table of contents, photographs, captions, and bold words. Did these text features give you any information or predictions about what you will read in this book?

Vocabulary: *Vocabulary Is Key to Reading Comprehension*

Use the following directions to prompt a conversation about each word.

- Read the vocabulary words.
- What comes to mind when you see each word?
- What do you think each word means?

Vocabulary Words:

- *armor*
- *asteroid*
- *club*
- *continent*
- *fossils*
- *habitat*
- *lizard*
- *osteoderm*
- *plates*
- *surroundings*

During Reading: *Reading for Meaning and Understanding*

To achieve deep comprehension of a book, children are encouraged to use close reading strategies. During reading, it is important to have children stop and make connections. These connections result in deeper analysis and understanding of a book.

Close Reading a Text

During reading, have children stop and talk about the following:

- Any confusing parts
- Any unknown words
- Text to text, text to self, text to world connections
- The main idea in each chapter or heading

Encourage children to use context clues to determine the meaning of any unknown words. These strategies will help children learn to analyze the text more thoroughly as they read.

When you are finished reading this book, turn to the next-to-last page for **Text-Dependent Questions** and an **Extension Activity**.

TABLE OF CONTENTS

DISCOVERING *ANKYLOSAURUS*

Every summer Barnum Brown went out to dig for new bones. He wanted to find some new **fossils**. Brown worked for the American Museum of Natural History. The people there wanted to show the fossils at their museum in New York.

In 1906, Brown went back to Hell Creek. Four years earlier he found the first *Tyrannosaurus rex (T. rex)* bones there. It had taken his crew three summers to dig them up.

"Mr. Bones"

Barnum Brown started collecting fossils as a boy. He found them near his home in Kansas. Brown became a dinosaur hunter when he grew up. The newspapers called him "Mr. Bones."

Hell Creek was in Montana. That was a long way from New York City. Brown had to travel across the country by train. He took his assistant with him. Peter Kaisen also worked at the American Museum of Natural History.

Everyone on the crew was looking for a new find. That summer, it was Kaisen who made the big discovery. He found some new bones. They didn't look like any bones that had been found before. This creature seemed to be covered with **armor**. Its skull was the shape of a triangle!

A New Dinosaur Name

When Brown discovered the first *T. rex*, the president of the museum named it. This time, it was Brown's turn to name the new dinosaur. He called it *Ankylosaurus magniventris*. The word *Ankylosaurus* means "fused **lizard**." That is what the armor looked like. The massive size was shown in the second name. The word *magniventris* means "great belly."

MORE BONES

Brown named *Ankylosaurus* in 1908. As time went by, it became clear that more parts of this dinosaur were already back at the museum. In 1900, Brown had found armored **plates** in Wyoming. They were mixed with the bones of a *T. rex*.

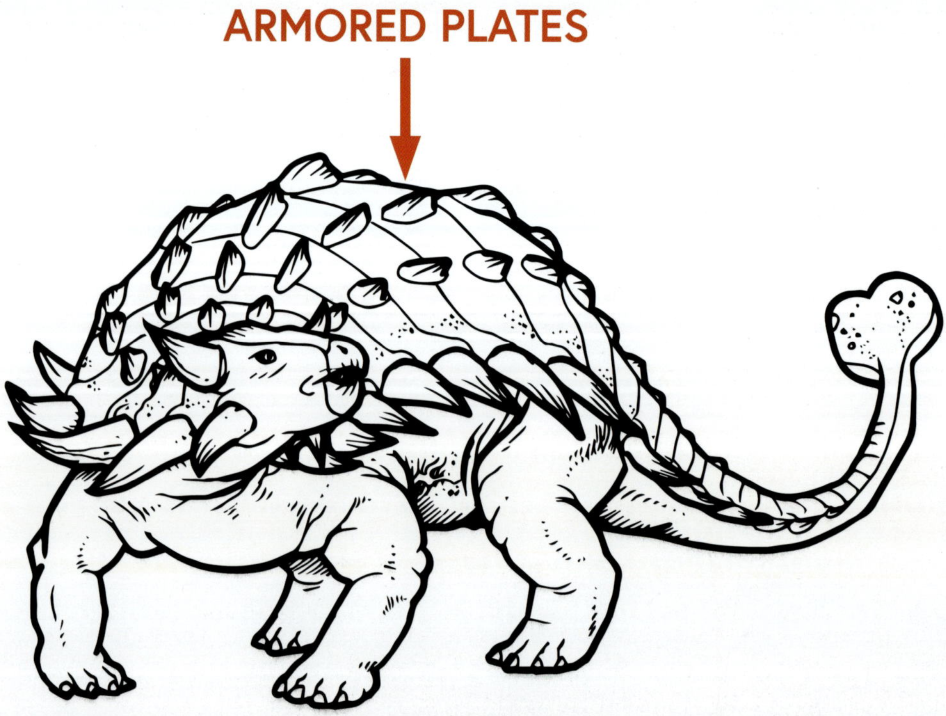

Fossil Hunters

Fossil hunters travel great distances to dig up fossils around the world. Women and men study plants and animals buried deep in the rocks. This is the science of paleontology.

Paleontology is not simple. It is not easy. It takes time to find the fossils. It also takes time for scientists to figure out what they found.

CLUB

In 1910, Brown and Kaisen found another *Ankylosaurus*. This time they were looking for fossils by the Red Deer River. They were in Alberta, Canada.

Each time they made a discovery, they found more. The first time, Brown only found armored plates near another dinosaur. In the second discovery, Kaisen found armored plates, parts of the triangular skull, two teeth, and some bones. This third time, the two men found even more. They found more bones. They found a complete skull. They also found a tail shaped like a **club**. It is the only *Ankylosaurus* tail that has ever been found.

COVERED WITH ARMOR

Ankylosaurus was an armored dinosaur. The top of its body was covered with armored plates. These plates were flat bones that joined together. It had bands of flat, bony plates. They were fused together.

Some of these flat plates also had spikes on top. There were rows of spikes on top of this dinosaur's body. It also had horns on the top and the sides of its head.

Even the eyes were protected. When this dinosaur closed its eyes, two eyelids made of bony armor came down.

Ankylosaurus had a short neck. Its small head was shaped like a triangle. There was only room for a tiny brain. Some scientists think its brain was no bigger than a golf ball.

At this time, there is no way to know what color *Ankylosaurus* was. Experts think it was probably dark green or brown. That way it would blend in with the trees, shrubs, and other plant life in its **habitat**.

Osteoderm

The fancy name for an armored plate is **osteoderm**. The word *osteo* means "bone." The second part of the word shows you where the bones were. The word *derm* means "skin." There are other animals with bones in their skin that are still alive. An armadillo is covered with body armor. So are alligators and crocodiles.

Ankylosaurus was as tall as an adult elephant. It was six feet (two meters) tall at the hip. But the rest of this dinosaur was much, much bigger. It was as wide as it was tall. It was also 33 feet (ten meters) long. This massive dinosaur weighed four tons (3,629 kilograms).

Everything on top of this massive dinosaur was covered with armor. Underneath it was not. This dinosaur had a "great belly." That was part of its name. But the belly was soft. It was not covered with armor. It was like a porcupine's belly.

Ankylosaurus moved slowly through its habitat on four short, broad legs. Its back legs were longer than its front legs. There were five toes on each of its stubby feet. These legs and feet were perfectly made to balance the creature's weight. Many scientists think *Ankylosaurus* might have looked like an armored tank rolling through its **surroundings**.

As it plodded along, *Ankylosaurus* swung its long, strong tail. At the end of the tail was a heavy club made of bone. This club could both frighten and fight off enemies. It was this dinosaur's main weapon. And it probably worked very well!

LIFE IN THE HERD

The sandy land where *Ankylosaurus* roamed was full of plant life. This gentle dinosaur was a plant eater. It lived in groups, or herds, near rivers and streams where it found its food.

Ankylosaurus ate tender, low-lying plants. It probably liked to munch on leaves, buds, and berries.

Inside its mouth was a jagged row of leaf-shaped teeth. These teeth were too weak to do much chewing. That's why experts think *Ankylosaurus* had a special stomach that broke down its food.

Predators

Few creatures posed a threat to an adult *Ankylosaurus*. But a mother would have to protect her young. She could use her bony tail club to fight.

There were meat-eating dinosaurs that lived nearby. *T. rex* shared the same habitat. This is why their bones were found together in 1900.

Scientists think most dinosaurs laid eggs in nests. They dug these shallow nests in the ground. An *Ankylosaurus* may have guarded its eggs until they hatched.

An *Ankylosaurus* mother probably fed her babies with her beak. She gave them berries and seeds until they were able to find their own food.

EXTINCT!

Ankylosaurus was one of the last dinosaurs on Earth. So far, all of their bones have been found near the Rocky Mountains. These mountains are now surrounded by land. They are in the middle of the North American **continent**. But long ago, these mountains were near a saltwater sea. *Ankylosaurus* lived nearby on the hot, wet plains.

Ankylosaurs

The *Ankylosaurus* was a rare dinosaur. To this day, very few of these dinosaurs have been found. But fossils of other dinosaurs like them have been discovered. These other dinosaurs also had armored plates. They were also long, low, and wide. This group of dinosaurs was named ankylosaurs.

Why did all of the *Ankylosauruses* die? How did they become extinct? Some experts think an **asteroid** hit Earth 65 million years ago. The asteroid would have caused a huge explosion. Then a huge black cloud of dust might have blocked all the sunlight. This would have wiped out many life-forms. Many plants, mammals, sea creatures, and dinosaurs were gone forever.

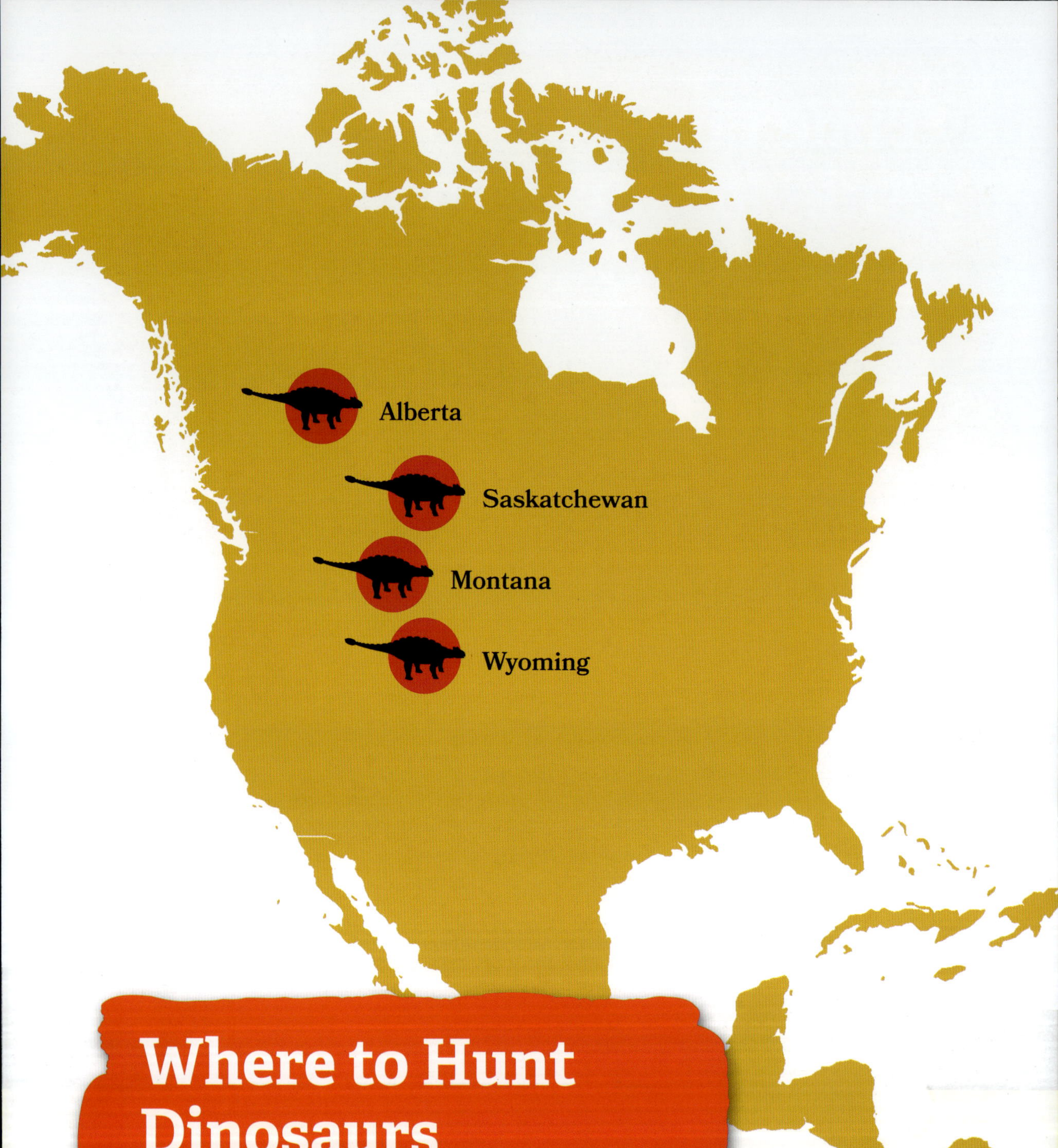

Where to Hunt Dinosaurs

Ankylosaurus fossils have been found in the western United States and Canada. They were found in Alberta, Saskatchewan, Montana, and Wyoming.

Time Line: *Ankylosaurus* and You

Do you see yourself on the time line? Look at the far right. You live in the Quaternary Period of the Cenozoic Era. Dinosaurs lived in the era before ours. They roamed Earth in the Mesozoic Era.

The Mesozoic Era had three time periods. *Ankylosaurus* lived in the last one. It was a Cretaceous dinosaur. It lived on Earth 67 to 65 million years ago.

MESOZOIC			CENOZOIC	
Triassic	**Jurassic**	**Cretaceous**	**Tertiary**	**Quaternary**
251–199.6 million years ago	**199.6–145.5** million years ago	**145.5–65.5** million years ago	**65.5–1.81** million years ago	**1.81–NOW** million years ago

GLOSSARY

armor (AHR-mur): a covering worn to protect a person or an animal in battle

asteroid (AS-tuh-roid): a rock in space

club (khlub): a thick, heavy stick or bone used as a weapon

continent (KAHN-tuh-nuhnt): one of Earth's seven large land masses: Asia, Africa, Europe, North America, South America, Australia, and Antarctica

fossils (FAH-suhls): the remains or imprints of an ancient animal or plant found in rock

habitat (HAB-i-tat): the place where a plant or animal lives

lizard (LIZ-urd): a reptile with a backbone that has four legs, scaly skin, and a long tail

osteoderm (AHS-tee-oh-durm): an armored plate of bone under the skin

plates (playts): flat sheets of bone or another hard material

surroundings (suh-ROUN-dingz): places around someone or something

INDEX

TEXT-DEPENDENT QUESTIONS

1. Why did the scientists go to Hell Creek?
2. Explain why the bones found at Red Deer River were so important.
3. Which of the *Ankylosaurus*'s body parts was not protected?
4. Why do experts think *Ankylosaurus* had a special stomach?
5. What might have happened if a *T. rex* attacked this dinosaur or its babies?

EXTENSION ACTIVITY

Practice your paleontology skills! Compare a turtle to an *Ankylosaurus*. Make a museum exhibit showing how they are alike and how they are different. Use words and images to explain the facts.

ABOUT THE AUTHOR

Anastasia Suen is the author of more than 300 books for young readers. Her children were both dinosaur fans, so she took them to the Natural History Museum of Los Angeles County and the La Brea Tar Pits often. They called both of these sites the "dinosaur" museum!

www.rourkeeducationalmedia.com

PHOTO CREDITS: Cover and Title Page ©Lady-Photo; Pg 5 ©American Museum of Natural History Library; Pg 6 ©Tim Evanson @ Wiki; Pg 7 ©Francois Gohier; Pg 9 ©Akkharat Jarusilawong; Pg 10 ©Vorobiov Oleksii 8, William Diller Matthew; Pg 13 ©Suwatwongkham; Pg 15 ©Daniel Eskridge; Pg 17 ©Jan Sovak; Pg 19 ©Daniel Eskridge; Pg 20 ©Barnum Brown; Pg 21 ©Daniel Eskridge; Pg 23, 24 ©CoreyFord; Pg 25 ©skiserge1; Pg 26 ©Zloyel; Pg 28, 29 ©Bryan Loh; Pg 29 ©ChrisGorgio

Edited by: Kim Thompson
Cover design by: Rhea Magaro-Wallace
Interior design by: Janine Fisher

Library of Congress PCN Data

Ankylosaurus / Anastasia Suen
(North American Dinosaurs)
ISBN 978-1-73161-448-3 (hard cover)
ISBN 978-1-73161-243-4 (soft cover)
ISBN 978-1-73161-553-4 (e-Book)
ISBN 978-1-73161-658-6 (ePub)
Library of Congress Control Number: 2019932148

Rourke Educational Media
Printed in the United States of America,
North Mankato, Minnesota